EARLY JAZZ FO

FINGERSTYLE GUITAR

BY LASSE JOHANSSON

Online Audio   www.melbay.com/99245BCDEB

Audio Contents

1 Buddy Bolden Blues [1:22]	7 Royal Garden Blues [2:28]	13 Alligator Crawl [2:43]
2 Creole Belles-march & two-step [2:53]	8 Wild Cat Blues [3:13]	14 Feeling My Way [2:54]
3 Memphis Blues [2:28]	9 Russian Rag [3:37]	15 Little Rock Getaway [2:30]
4 Dixie Jass Band One-Step [2:24]	10 Jazz Me Blues [1:48]	16 Ain't Misbehavin' [2:16]
5 Livery Stable Blues [2:11]	11 Muskrat Ramble [1:52]	17 Hong Kong Blues [2:33]
6 Don't You Leave Me Here [2:22]	12 Tia Juana [1:56]	

Recording engineer for the audio is Thomas Oberg.

1 2 3 4 5 6 7 8 9 0

Visit us on the Web at www.melbay.com — E-mail us at email@melbay.com

I am deeply grateful to Tom Thomason for his assistance in editing the text and notation material in this book.
And a special thanks to Ágnes, for her support throughout this project.

TABLE OF CONTENTS

INTRODUCTION

In the 60's, a number of fingerstyle guitarists started to arrange classic piano ragtime for the guitar. The alternating bass patterns, almost synonymous with the term fingerpicking, worked very well as the guitarists tried to evoke the left hand work of the ragtime pianists. Many folk guitarists tried their talents on these fingerpicking gems and the arrangements often stood out as real showpieces in their fingerstyle repertoire.

Rags for guitar weren't really a new thing, bluesmen like Blind Blake, Big Bill Broonzy and the Rev. Gary Davis had tried their hand at playing ragtime-like chord progressions and rhythms as far back as the 1920's. This was the blues but it had a ragtime flavor and guitarists played it fingerstyle.

As the folk revival of the 60's re-discovered these old blues masters, guitarists like Dave Laibman, Eric Shoenberg and Dave van Ronk dug deeply into the piano scores and came up with something different, real classic ragtime for the guitar.

I tried it myself and arranged a variety of rags for solo and duet guitars that resulted in several albums on the Kicking Mule label. To develop my arranging skills and move on to another area of music that wasn't too far afield from ragtime, I looked into early jazz music. When the ragtime craze ended, jazz music was knocking at the door, so there are many similarities between classic ragtime and early jazz. Many of the pioneer jazz pianists played ragtime and the syncopated rhythms, on top of the steady bass, found big-band settings in early brassbands at the turn of the century. These brass bands, ragtime piano and, of course, the ever-present blues became the cornerstones of what came to be called jazz.

In the latter part of the teens, the heavy two-beat march of classic ragtime had gradually changed. A more flowing rhythm was achieved by the more evenly accented 4/4 left hand work of, for instance, Jelly Roll Morton. When the great New York pianists, such as James P. Johnson, Willie "The Lion" Smith and Thomas "Fats" Waller, further developed the rhythms and harmonies in the 20's, ragtime was dead and a new pianostyle had taken its place: stride piano.

While looking for ways to arrange early jazz music for fingerstyle guitar, I could find few jazz guitarists that routinely played with their fingers. Nearly all of the early jazz guitarists, such as Eddie Lang, Dick McDonough, George van Eps and Carl Kress played with a plectrum. Lonnie Johnson stands out as being a guitarist that could master the blues and jazz idioms and play either with a plectrum or in a fingerpicking style.

Actually, the use of the guitar didn't appear in recorded jazz music at all until recording techniques made it possible. The first jazz bands had banjoists, not guitarists. The reason for this being that the volume of the banjo cut through the sound of horns and drums more easily. The invention of new microphones made the softer sounds of the guitar available on record years after the first jazz records had been made.

Another challenge, in arranging jazz for fingerstyle guitar, was finding a way to deal with the basis of all jazz music: improvisation. Since most early jazz music was played by bands, the soloists had a lot of back-up by accompanying musicians. The fingerstyle guitarist, on the other hand, is alone and has to provide his own accompaniment. This doesn't mean that there's no improvisation present in these arrangements. In arranging these tunes, I've listened to a lot of different recordings of them and I've often selected melodies and phrasings that were originally improvisations. But, in most cases I have concentrated on the beauty of the melodies and tried to portray them with respect, realizing that these are beautiful compositions, not just a bunch of chord progressions to be improvised around. I would, however, encourage guitarists to use my bass lines and fingerings and add some syncopations and notes of their own. That way the music will live and take color from whoever is doing the interpretation.

I don't think you can really compare these arrangements with the way any of these tunes would have been played on other instruments. I'm not trying to sound like a piano player and there's no way a solo guitar could evoke the sounds of a whole jazz band. The simplest way to express it would be to say that I've approached the music as a fingerstyle guitarist would have and the result is - *Early Jazz for Fingerstyle Guitar*.

The music that I've put together here is a collection of jazz spanning from the turn of the last century up until the 1930's. Work on the earliest arrangements in this book started in the middle of the 70's while most are done as recently as the turn of the millenium. I've included two ragtime numbers, *Russian Rag* and *Creole Belles - march & two-step*. You'll find arrangements of both sides of the first jazz record by the Original Dixieland Jazz Band as well as two vocal blues by Jelly Roll Morton. Bix Beiderbecke is the inspiration for two more numbers, *Jazz Me Blues* and *Tia Juana*, both recorded by him in 1924. We know that *Royal Garden Blues* was published in 1919 but the origins of *Muskrat Ramble* are more obscure, even though Kid Ory claims he wrote it in 1926. W.C Handy's *Memphis Blues* was published in 1912, one of the first times the word "blues" appears on a sheet-music cover. The 1923 hit *Wild Cat Blues* launched the career of Sidney Bechet. *Alligator Crawl* and *Ain't Misbehavin'*, by Thomas "Fats" Waller, first saw the light of day in the latter part of the 20's. At the end the collection I have turned to the 30's with pieces by Joe Sullivan and Hoagy Carmichael. *Feeling My Way* is a beautiful tune by one of the very first jazz guitarists, Eddie Lang. It was originally played as a duet with Carl Kress on second guitar. I found it thrilling to hear these great guitarists taking turns playing melody and rhythm. The sound is almost like fingerstyle guitar except that there are two guitars playing.

Hope you like it.
Lasse Johansson

Photo by Ágnes Murányi.

Lasse Johansson

BIOGRAPHY

Lars "Lasse" Johansson started playing fingerpicking guitar in the style of Doc Watson and Merle Travis in the mid 60's.

He soon started arranging for the guitar and recorded his first fingerstyle arrangement, Scott Joplin's Maple Leaf Rag, in 1969.

In 1970 he met Stefan Grossman and signed with Kicking Mule Records to record his duet and solo guitar arrangements of classic ragtime. The first album to be released was *March and Two Step-ragtime guitar duets*, featuring his duet partner Claes Palmkvist.

In the 70's, Lars and Claes went on to record many tunes that appeared in anthologies on the Kicking Mule label. The music was mainly classic piano ragtime from the beginning of the last century.

King Porter Stomp, an album of arrangements of "Jelly Roll" Morton's music, was recorded in1980.

Samples of Lars' work now began to appear in the "Stefan Grossman's Guitar Workshop" collections of fingerstyle guitar arrangements published by Mel Bay.

In 1994 Mel Bay published a book entitled *The Music of Jelly Roll Morton* containing the arrangements from the *King Porter Stomp* album.

Lars then began teaching, and performing, fingerstyle guitar and has continued to do so into the new millenium.

Other Mel Bay books - featuring several of Johansson's arrangements

MB 94082   Ragtime Guitar
MB 94505   Classic Ragtime Guitar Solos
MB 94561   Mel Bay's Complete Fingerstyle Guitar Book
MB 95268   The Classic Rags of Scott Joplin
MB 95267   The Music of Jelly Roll Morton for Fingerstyle Guitar
MB 99633   Mel Bay's Master Anthology of Fingerstyle Guitar Solos vol. 2

DISCOGRAPHY
            Kicking Mule Records
SNKF 117   Novelty Guitar Instrumentals
SNKF 120   March and Two-Step
SNKF 130   Masters of the Ragtime Guitar
SNKF 135   Advanced Fingerpicking Guitar Techniques
SNKF 169   King Porter Stomp
            Shanachie-CD:s
98013/14   Fingerpicking Guitar Delights
98015/16   The Entertainer

NOTATION, TABLATURE
AND SOME PLAYING TECHNIQUES

Here are some illustrations of the special effects used in these arrangements.

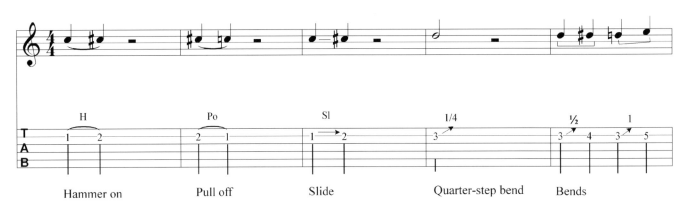

Hammer on   Pull off   Slide   Quarter-step bend   Bends

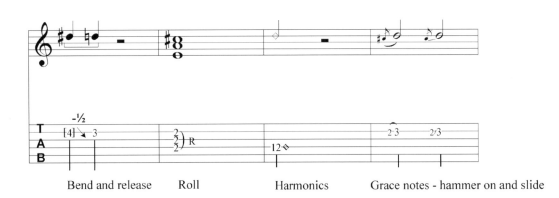

Bend and release   Roll   Harmonics   Grace notes - hammer on and slide

This symbol shows that the melody should be played with a triplet feel, in a more "swinging" rhythm than the straight 1/8 notes indicate.

Most of the time these arrangements have a steady alternating bass line. This is played with the thumb of your picking hand. Most notes played with the thumb have the stems in the notation pointing downwards.

I use my left-hand thumb for most fingerings on the sixth string. I also occasionally use my left-hand thumb on the fifth string.

As often as possible I hold down whole chord shapes with my left hand to get a bigger sound out of the guitar. This means that sometimes I fret strings that are not actually being played, so check out the chords indicated above the tablature.

Sometimes I fret two strings with one finger, placing the finger between the strings in order to fret both of them. This technique enables me to more freely use my other fingers for the melody.

I never use full barre chords, but often partial barre chords on the treble strings.

Editor's note: Blank tab stems indicate a rest or tie.

BUDDY BOLDEN BLUES

Key of C

"Buddy Bolden Blues" is definitely one of the oldest of jazz tunes. Jelly Roll Morton remembers hearing it being played by Buddy Bolden himself in New Orleans in the very first years of the 20th century but it's origins are probably much earlier. Buddy Bolden, by many considered to be the leader of the very first jazz band, called the tune "Funky Butt".

Barney and Seymore used a similar theme in their ragtime piano piece "St. Louis Tickle". Jelly Roll Morton accused Barney and Seymore of stealing the theme from Bolden but, as with many other jazz themes, it's not easy to name the originator. It was a popular folk tune at the turn of the century and also appeared in Scott Joplin's "Sarah Dear", Ben Harney's "The Cakewalk in the Sky" as well as Louis Chauvin's ballad "Babe, It's Too Long Off".

"St. Louis Tickle" was, in the early 60's, turned into a ragtime guitar number by singer-guitarist Dave van Ronk. His version of "St. Louis Tickle" is a classic in the area of ragtime guitar and one of the very first piano rags arranged for guitar.

I play it as a slow blues in the key of C. It's basically a one-theme tune with variations. Jelly Roll Morton could probably play this tune all night with different variations each time 'round. I do two variations, the first contains some licks that Jelly Roll used to play and the second is more my own. Part of this arrangement was recorded on the LP *King Porter Stomp* - Kicking Mule SNKF 169.

The legendary Buddy Bolden's band. Buddy Bolden is standing behind the guitarist. Other members include trombonist Willie Cornish and clarinetist Frank Lewis.

1. BUDDY BOLDEN BLUES

Trad.

Guitar arrangement by Lasse Johansson

CREOLE BELLES - MARCH & TWO-STEP

Key of G - trio in C

"Creole Belles" is a cakewalk written by composer J. Bodewalt Lampe in the year 1900. Lyrics were added to the middle section and it became a popular song of it's day. The country-blues guitarist Mississippi John Hurt eventually turned this part of the composition into a song which he used to play and sing: "My Creole Belle". This has since become a standard tune in the field of folk-blues guitar.

I play all three sections. The first section has a brass band feeling to it, which comes as no surprise as "Creole Belles" was one of the early cakewalks that the great bandmaster John Phillip Sousa included in his repertoire when looking for new syncopated rhythms. The second section is the song "My Creole Belle" and the third a trio in a different key.

An earlier version of this arrangement was recorded on *Masters of the Ragtime Guitar*-Kicking Mule SNKF 130 and later re-released as *Fingerpicking Guitar Delights* -Shanachie 98013/14.

2. CREOLE BELLES - MARCH & TWO-STEP

J Bodewalt Lampe

Guitar arrangement by Lasse Johansson

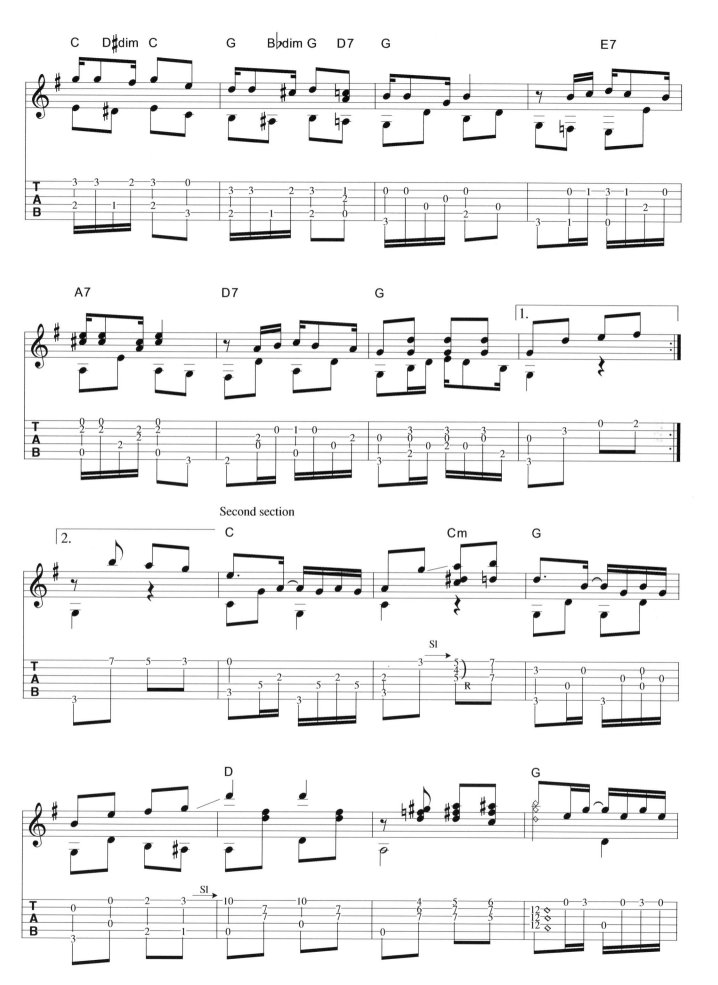

Second section

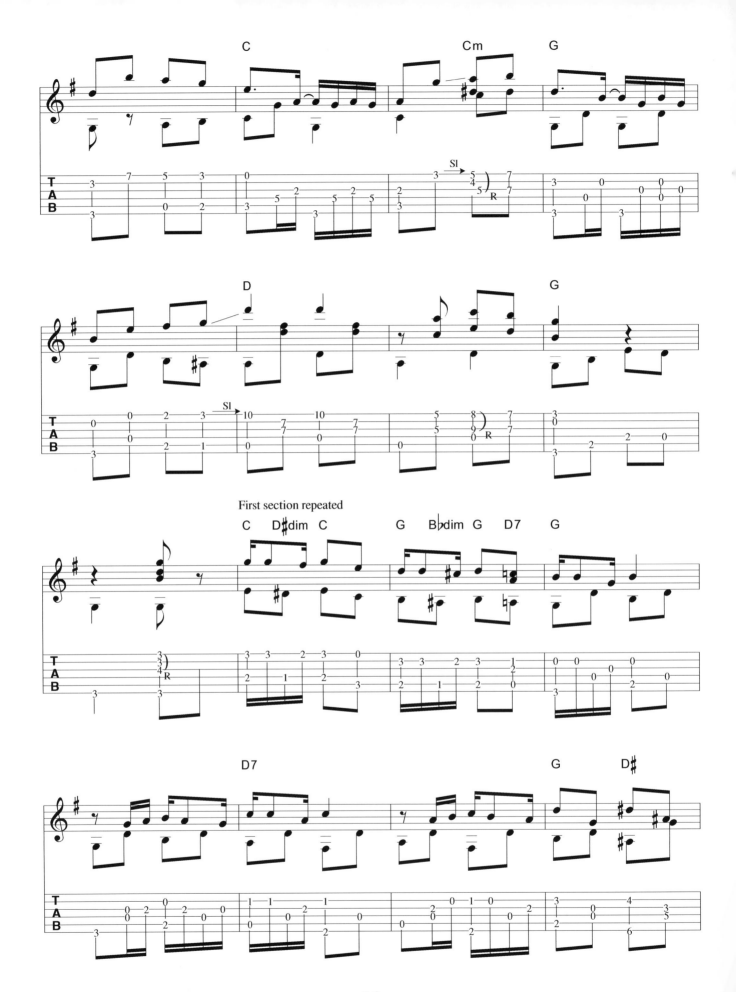

First section repeated

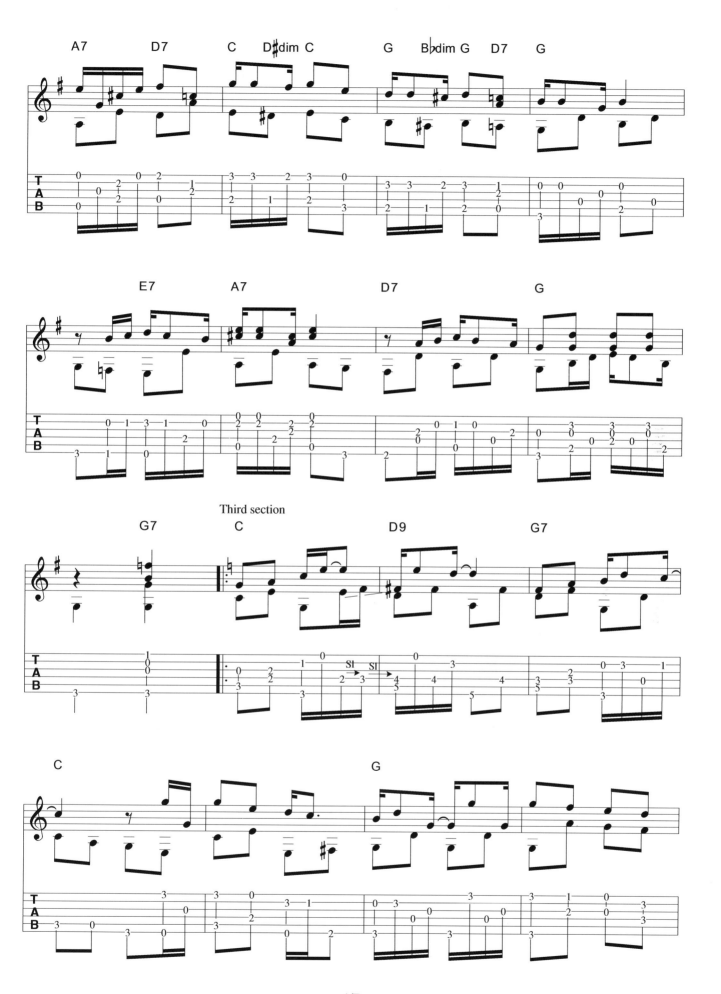

Third section

MEMPHIS BLUES

Key of A - verse in C

"Memphis Blues" is one of the first compositions by W.C. Handy. It was probably also the very first composition to have been published with the word "Blues" in the title. Handy composed the tune at the request of a certain E.H. Crump in order to help him in his bid for mayor of Memphis in 1909. The original title was "Mr. Crumb" but Handy changed the title to "Memphis Blues" when he registered a piano version for copyright in 1910.

My first and second sections are based on the Original Memphis Five version and the arrangement of the third section pays tribute to country-guitarist Arthel "Doc" Watson who recorded his version of "Memphis Blues" in the 70's.

The Original Memphis Five including (left to right) Phil Napoleon, Frank Signorelli, Miff Mole and clarinetist Jimmy Lytell.

3. MEMPHIS BLUES

W.C. Handy

Guitar arrangement by Lasse Johansson

* Blank tab stems indicate a rest or tie.

Second section

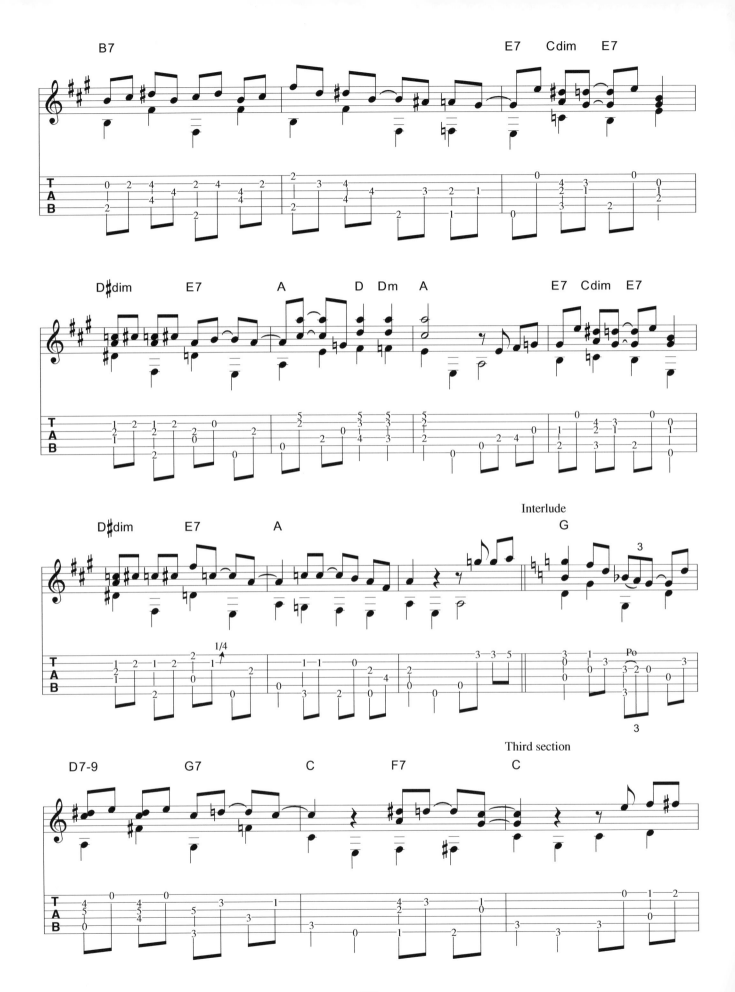

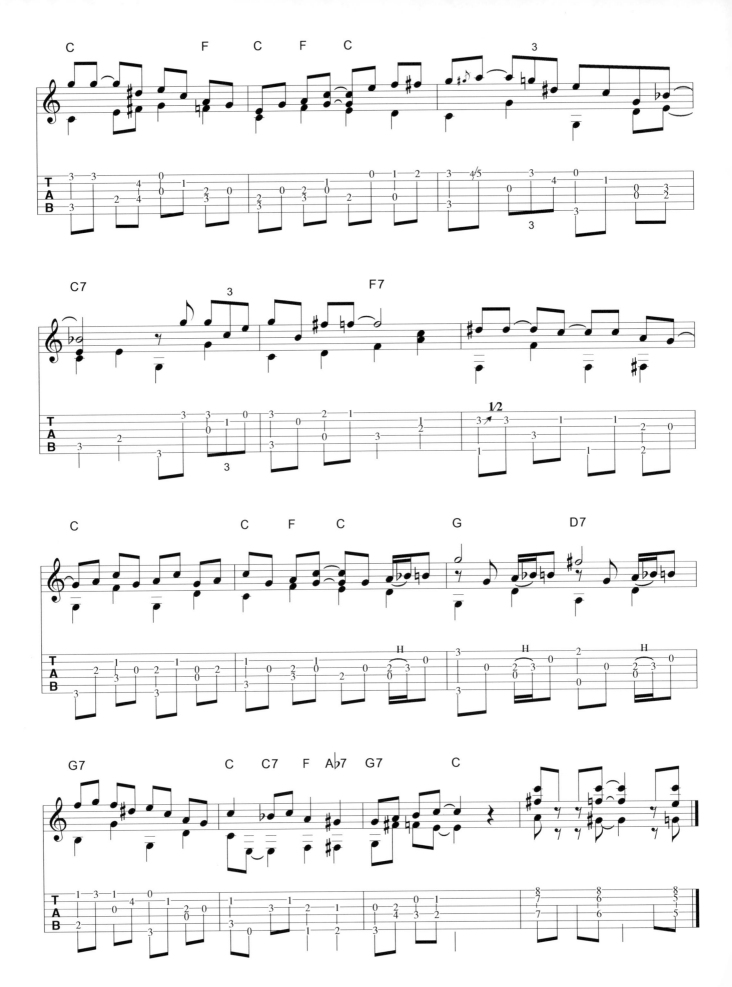

24

DIXIE JASS BAND ONE-STEP

Key of D - G , That Teasin' Rag in C

The all white Original Dixieland Jazz Band was given opportunity to do the first jazz recording in 1917. Nick la Rocca, the hornplayer, claimed that he and the band had invented "jass" and for a while those that only knew jazz from listening to records believed him. "Dixie Jass Band One-Step" was teamed up with "Livery Stable Blues" on that very first jazz release. It is, however, interesting to note that the ODJB had recorded "(Back Home Again in) Indiana" and "Darktown Strutter's Ball" a month earlier but this recording was rejected for lack of commercial potential. After the success of "Dixie Jass Band One-Step"/"Livery Stable Blues" that first recording was rushed out onto the market.

The third section was not written by the band, it's actually a ragtime song - "That Teasin' Rag" - written by Joe Jordan in 1909. When Jordan heard the Victor recording by ODJB he sued them and the records where withdrawn and re-labeled. The new label read - "Dixie Jass Band One-Step", introducing "That Teasin' Rag" by Joe Jordan. Joe Jordan was a ragtime pianist, bandleader, multi-instrumentalist and arranger. In 1905 he organized the Memphis Students a group that, according to James Weldon Johnson, was the first jazz band ever heard on a New York stage.

In 1938 the Original Dixieland Jazz Band regrouped and cut a revival record, renaming this piece the "Original Dixieland Jazz Band One-Step" - the credit to Joe Jordan long forgotten.

My arrangement comes right out of listening to the original recording by the band. All sections are in different keys and the last section is Joe Jordan's "That Teasin' Rag".

An earlier version of this arrangement was recorded on *Masters of Ragtime Guitar* - Kicking Mule SNKF 130 and later re-released on *Fingerpicking Guitar Delights*-Shanachie 98013/14.

The original Original Dixieland Jazz Band. Tony Spargo, Eddie Edwards, Nick la Rocca, Alcide Nunez and Henry Ragas.

4. DIXIE JASS BAND ONE-STEP

D.J. (Nick) La Rocca

Guitar arrangement by Lasse Johansson

Third section

28

29

LIVERY STABLE BLUES

Key of E

The Original Dixieland Jazz Band had a clarinetist named Alphonse "Yellow" Nunez. Nunez was fired by the band before their first recording and was replaced by Larry Shields.

"Livery Stable Blues" was intended as the B-side of the first jazz record ever released but was such a hit at the time that it came to be regarded as the main title. The ODJB had the copyright for this tune under the name "Barnyard Blues" but, when the record came out, the name was changed to "Livery Stable Blues". Nunez, realizing that this tune, under it's new name, was without copyright, immediately filed for copyright. Nick la Rocca of the ODJB sued Nunez who, according to la Rocca, had nothing to do with composing this piece. The judge couldn't decide who had composed it and, thus, settle the argument. He ruled that both composers had the rights to the tune and added that, in his opinion, it was impossible to designate a specific composer for jazz music since it was all based on improvisations. Thus, this composition bears two names: Livery Stable Blues (by Nunez) and Barnyard Blues (by la Rocca). I have arranged it as a basic blues in the key of E.

The Original Dixieland Jazz Band. Tony Spargo, Eddie Edwards, Nick La Rocca, Larry Shields and J.Russell Robinson.

5. LIVERY STABLE BLUES

Ray Lopes-Alcide Nunez

Guitar arrangement by Lasse Johansson

First section   repeated

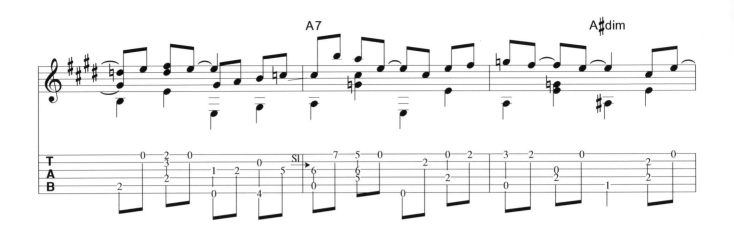

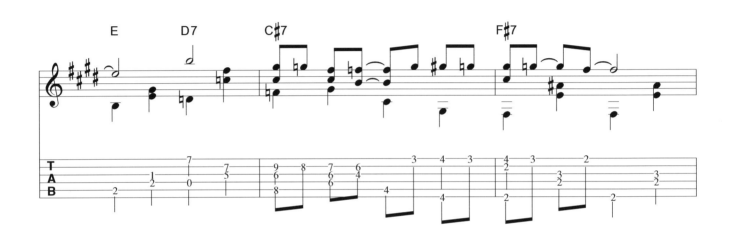

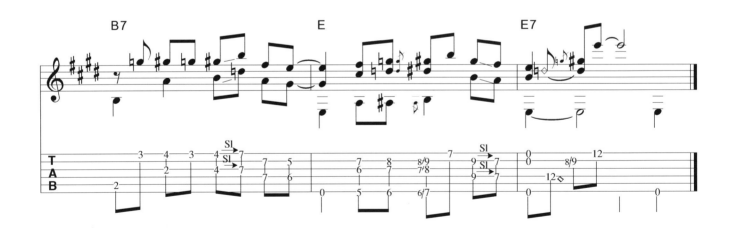

DON'T YOU LEAVE ME HERE

Key of A

This one is, once again, a jazz tune that folk guitarists like to play. Jorma Kaukonen and Hot Tuna did a version of it and I've also heard it with Jim Kweskin's Jug Band. It was recorded by Jelly Roll Morton in 1939 but the tune is probably much older than that.

My arrangement of the verse takes it's inspiration from many sources but the bridge is based on Jelly Roll Morton's solo on the Library of Congress recordings made by Alan Lomax. The first time the verse is played, it's a pretty straight-forward adaption of the melody and bass line, the second time around I've added more improvisational licks.

Ferdinand "Jelly-Roll" Morton

6. DON'T YOU LEAVE ME HERE

Jelly Roll Morton

Guitar arrangement by Lasse Johansson

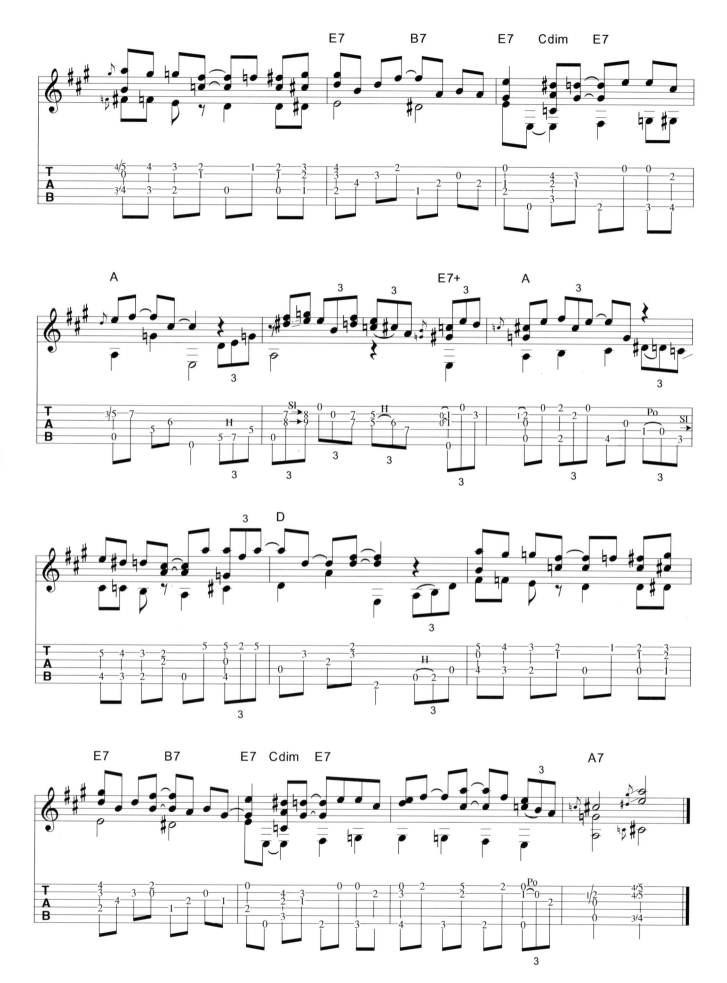

ROYAL GARDEN BLUES

Key of A and D

Clarence and Spencer Williams (no relation) published "Royal Garden Blues" in 1919 and it has become a standard dixieland piece. According to clarinetist Jimmi Noone, the actual composers were himself and King Oliver, who had sold it to Clarence Williams. The latter then, together with Spencer Williams, published it as their own composition.

The title refers to the Royal Gardens in Chicago, a dancehall where Oliver's Creole Jazz Band used to play, so perhaps King Oliver may have had something to do with it.

Clarence Williams band with Prince Robinson, Ed Allen and washboard player Floyd Casey.

7. ROYAL GARDEN BLUES

Clarence Williams-Spencer Williams

Guitar arrangement by Lasse Johansson

Introduction

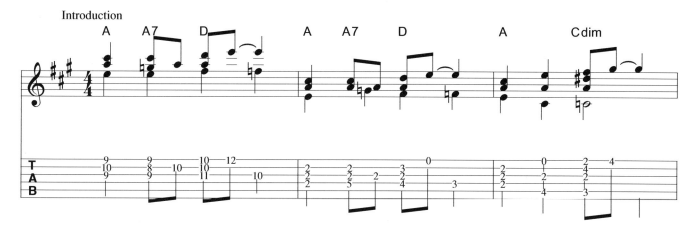

First section

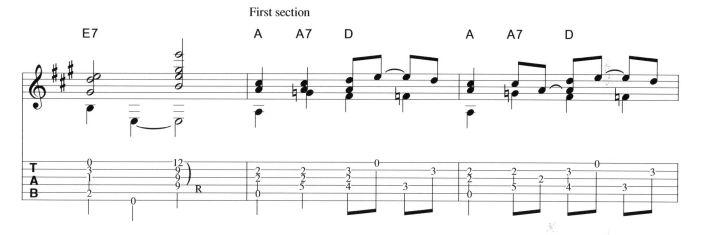

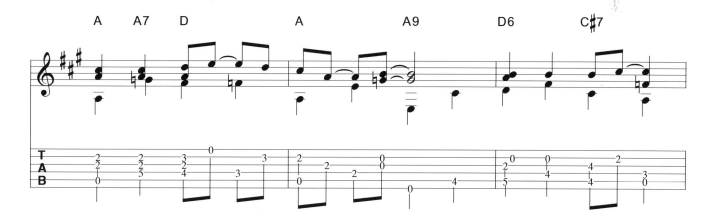

44

48

WILD CAT BLUES

Key of C, F and D min

A young, and still relatively unknown, Thomas "Fats" Waller in the early 20's recieved some help from Clarence Williams in completing a few ideas he had for new musical compositions. The first result of this collaboration was "Wild Cat Blues" which was published by Clarence Williams own publishing label. "Wild Cat Blues" seems to be the very first Waller composition to be published.

It was first recorded by Clarence William's Blue Five in 1923 and became an immediate hit. The powerful soprano sax playing of Sidney Bechet dominated this recording and it became the breakthrough of Bechet's long career.

My arrangement is a transcription of how the band played it on that 1923 record.

Thomas "Fats" Waller

8. WILD CAT BLUES

Fats Waller-Clarence Williams

Guitar arrangement by Lasse Johansson

Second section

First section repeated

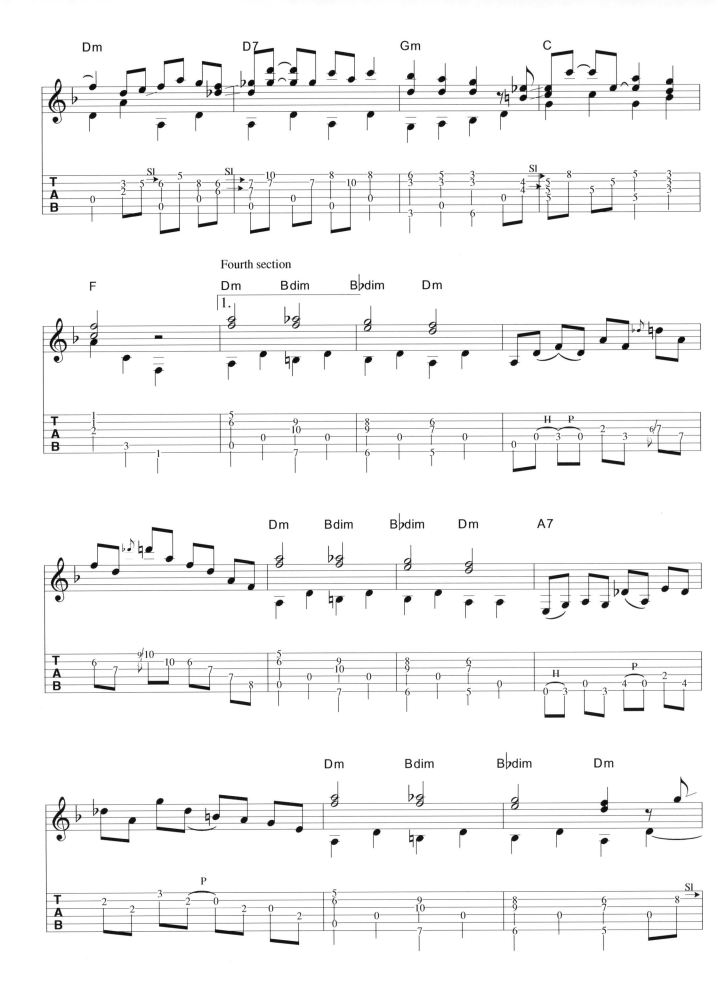

RUSSIAN RAG (ROCKIES' RAG)

Key of F - D minor

"Russian Rag" is a classic ragtime piano piece from 1918. What's so special about it is that the composer, George L.Cobb, in writing this piece incorporated the famous piano "Prelude" by russian composer Rachmaninoff in the opening section. This Rachmaninoff prelude has inspired several others to do their own versions. One of these was jazz guitarist Eddie Lang, represented in this collection by one of his own tunes, who arranged a version of it in 1929.

This arrangement is a straight classic ragtime arrangement, in which you try to fit all the keys of the piano and the ten fingers of the pianist to the six strings of the guitar.

An earlier version of this arrangement was recorded on *Masters of the Ragtime Guitar - Kicking Mule SNKF 130.*

9. RUSSIAN RAG

George L. Cobb

Interpolating the famous, "Prelude", by Rachmaninoff
Guitar arrangement by Lasse Johansson

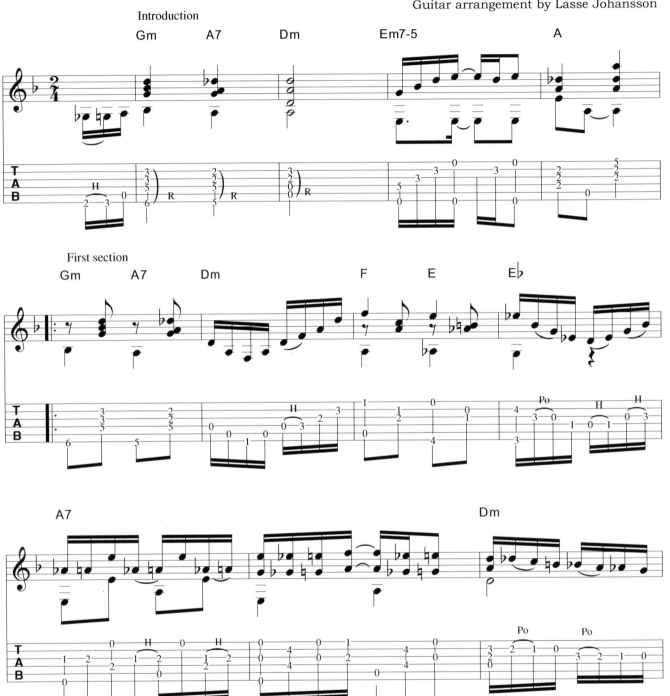

First section repeated

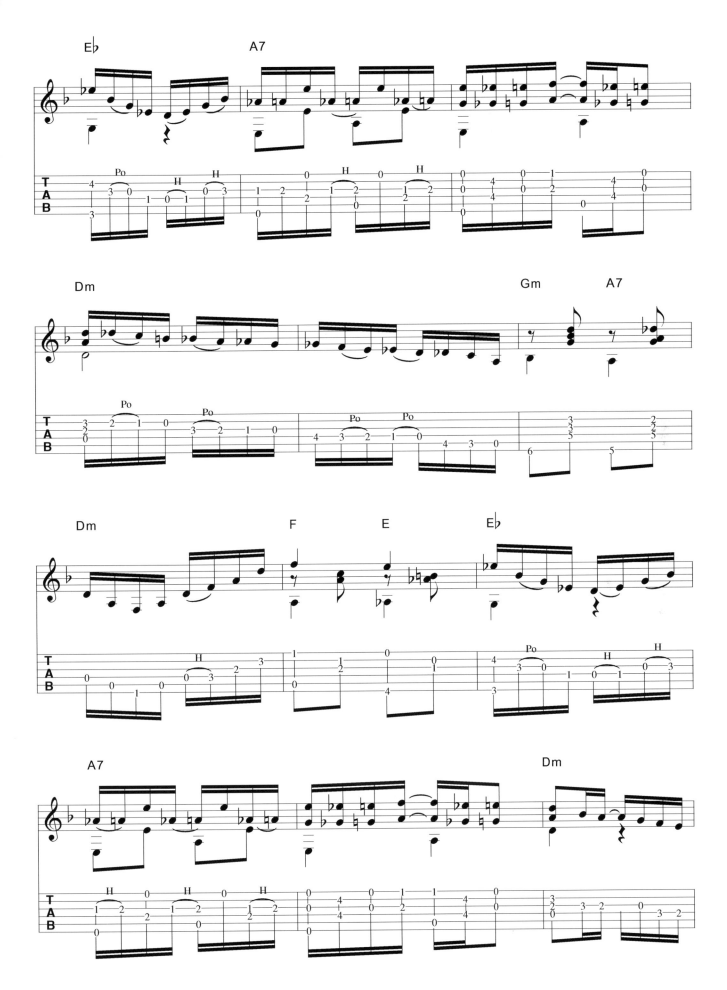

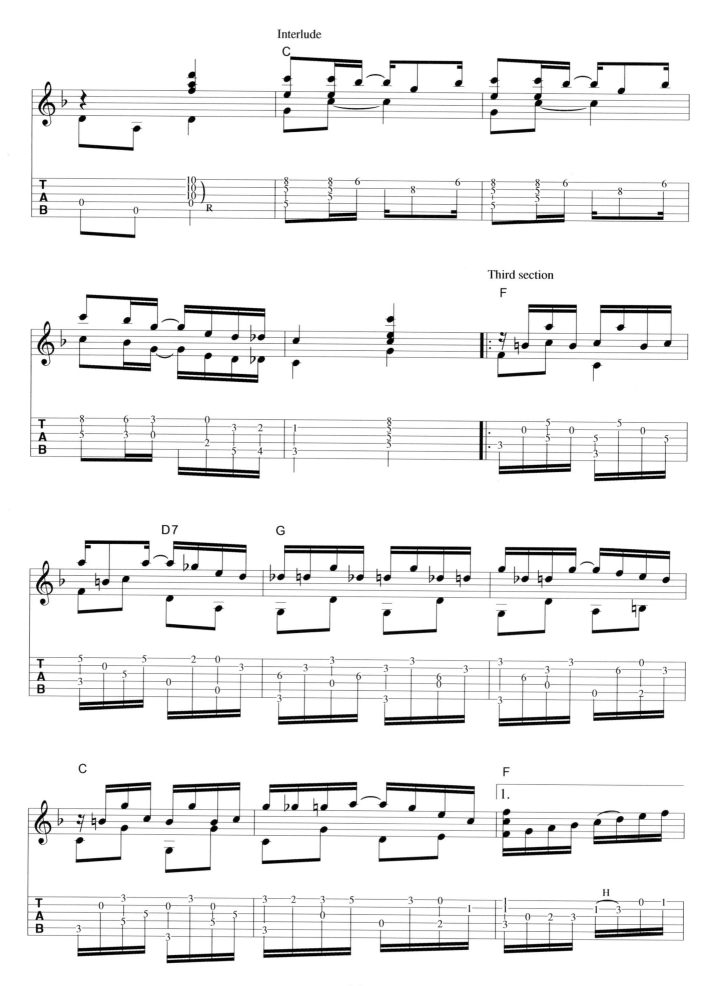

64

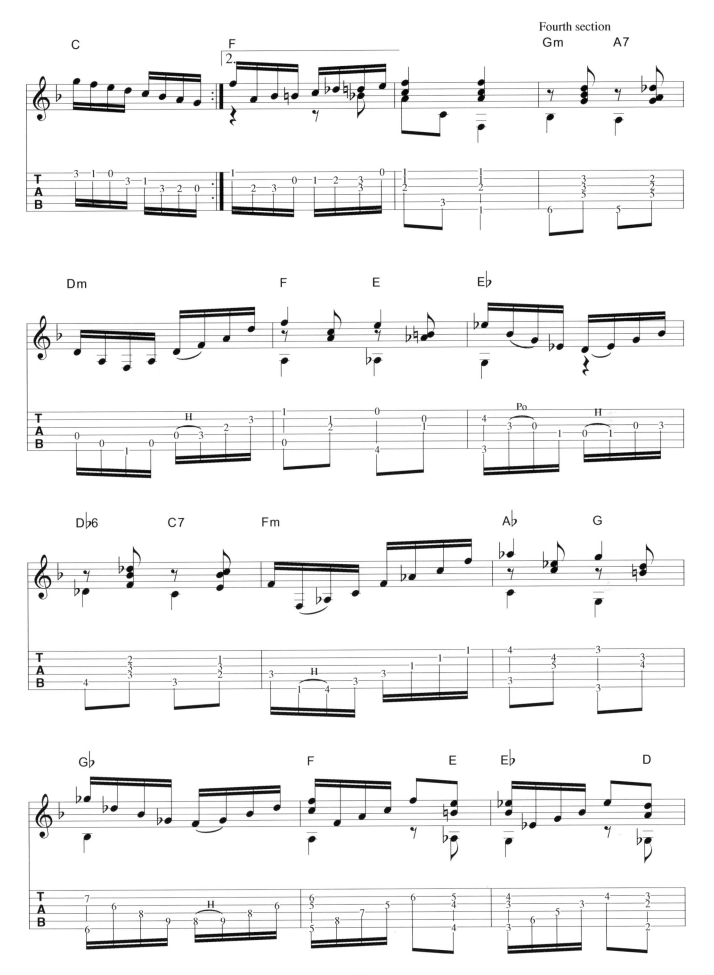

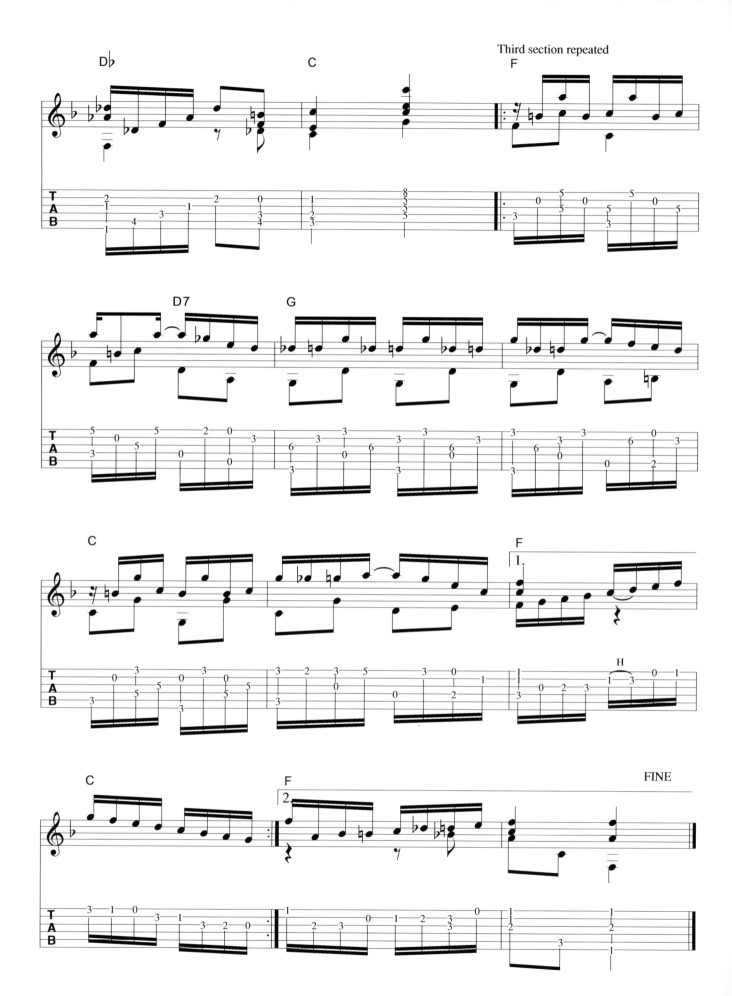

JAZZ ME BLUES

Key of C

This was written by Tom Delaney and first recorded in 1920 by Lucille Hegamin and again in 1921 by the Original Dixieland Jass Band. It was a very popular piece during the 20's, especially with the dance bands. Like guitarist Freddie Green (with Count Basie) and trumpeter Cat Andersson (with Duke Ellington), Tom Delaney grew up in the Jenkin's Orphanage Institute in Charleston, S.C., where music was an important part of the boy's education.

This tune was featured on Bix Beiderbecke's first recording with the The Wolverines. The record was cut in 1924 and marks the beginning of Bix's recording career.

My arrangements stems from listening to the Beiderbecke recording.

Bix Beiderbecke and the Wolverine Orchestra with (left to right) Vic Moore, George Johnson, Jimmy Hartwell, Bix, Al Grande, Min Leibrook, Bob Gillette and (standing) Dick Voynow.

10. JAZZ ME BLUES

Tom Delaney

Guitar arrangement by Lasse Johansson

First section repeated

MUSKRAT RAMBLE

Key of A

"Muskrat Ramble" was first recorded by Louis Armstrong's Hot Five in 1926. Edward "Kid" Ory, the band's trombone player, brought the tune to the recording session claiming he had written it.

It was later argued that "Muskrat Ramble" was not written by Ory at all. Many musicians remembered it as being played around New Orleans long before the Hot Five recorded it in the 20's. Sidney Bechet recalls a tune called "The Old Cow That Died" that was very similar.

Originally, this tune may have been called "Muscat Ramble", taking it's name from a type of wine that was popular around the New Orleans area at the turn of the century.

In the 60's Country Joe McDonald based his comment on the Vietnam war, "Fixing to Die Rag" on this tune, performing it with his band Country Joe & the Fish.

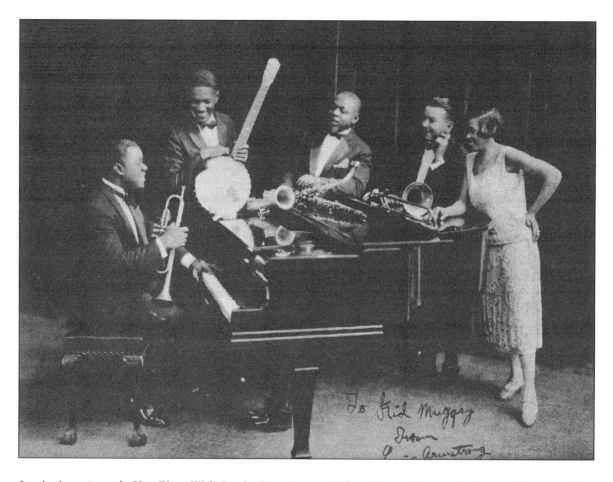

Louis Armstrong's Hot Five. With Louis Armstrong at the piano, Johnny St Cyr, Johnny Dodds, Kid Ory and Lil Hardin-Armstrong.

11. MUSKRAT RAMBLE

Edward "Kid" Ory

Guitar arrangement by Lasse Johansson

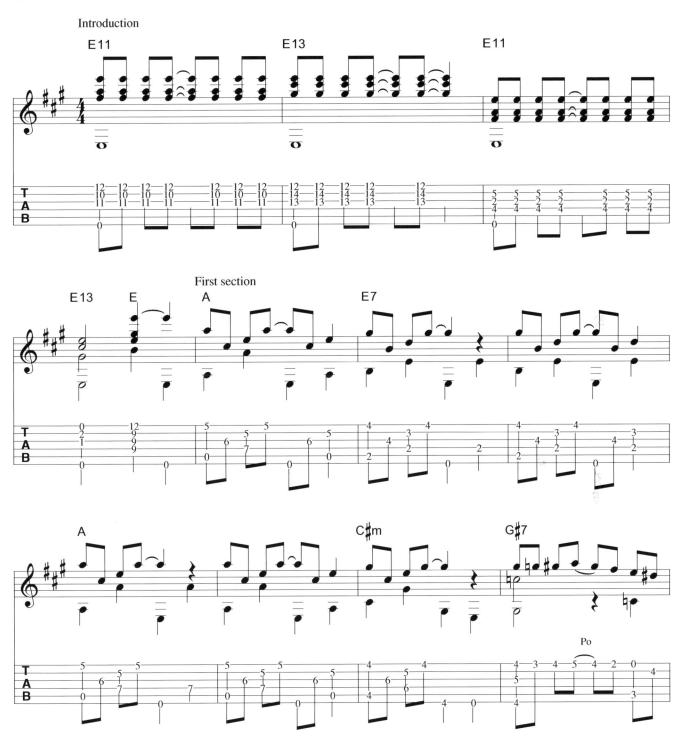

TIA JUANA

Key of G

Written by Larry Conley and Gene Rodemich, "Tia Juana" was first recorded by Gene Rodemich and his orchestra in 1924. It was recorded again in the same year by Bix Beiderbecke, on his last recording with the Wolverines. Ry Cooder did a version on his *Jazz* album, teaming it up with Morton's "The Pearls". My arrangement is a combination of a sheet-music transcription and listening to the Wolverines with Bix Beiderbecke.

The Wolverine Orchestra Dick Voynow, Bob Gillette, George Johnson, Min Leibrook, Vic Moore, Jimmy Hartwell and Bix Beiderbecke.

12. TIA JUANA

Conley-Rodemich

Guitar arrangement by Lasse Johansson

Second section

Third section

82

ALLIGATOR CRAWL

Key of D - dropped D-tuning

Alligator Crawl by Thomas Fats Waller, written in 1927. It is both a piano solo and a song with lyrics by Razaf and Davis. It was first recorded by Louis Armstrong and the same year by Fess Williams.

Earlier titles for this tune were *House Party Stomp* and *Charleston Stomp.*

Fats Waller and his Rhythm. Gene Sedric, Cedric Wallace, guitarist Al Casey and the Deep River Boys vocal quartet.

13. ALLIGATOR CRAWL

Thomas "Fats" Waller

Guitar arrangement by Lasse Johansson

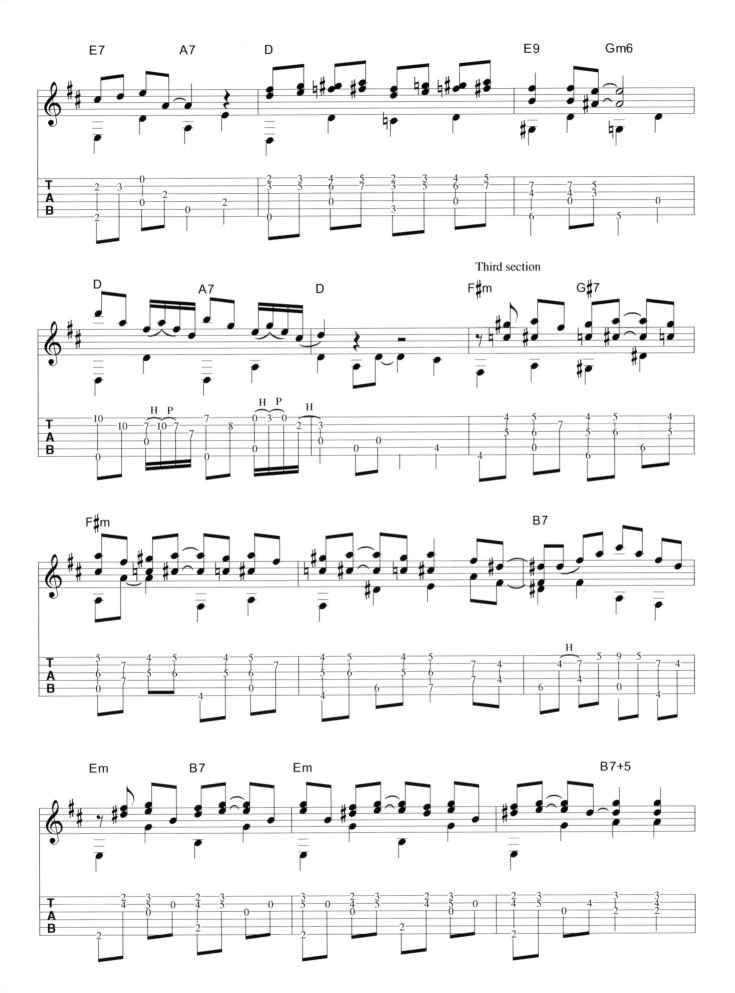

FEELING MY WAY

Key of A - F

Eddie Lang was one of the first, if not the very first, jazz guitarists. With early recording techniques, the only fretted instrument that could cut through the sound of trumpets and trombones was the banjo. In the 20's, the advent of new microphones changed recordings, making it possible for the more subtle tones of the guitar to be heard.

Eddie Lang first recorded in 1924 with the Mound City Blue Blowers. Violinist Joe Venuti was his partner but he also made several great guitar duet recordings with for instance Lonnie Johnson, Dick McDonough and Carl Kress, all pioneers of the jazz guitar. When he recorded with Lonnie Johnson, he had to assume the alias "Blind Willie" McDunn, to disguise the fact that it was a racially integrated session for the Okeh-2000 race records label.

"Feeling My Way" is a duet he recorded in 1932, the year before he died, with Carl Kress playing the chord line. I've taken the bass and chords of the back-up guitar and combined it with the single-string melody and turned it into a solo guitar arrangement.

The Mound City Blue Blowers. Dick Slevin, Jack Bland, Red McKenzie and on guitar Eddie Lang.

14. FEELING MY WAY

Eddie Lang

Guitar arrangement by Lasse Johansson

Second section

94

96

LITTLE ROCK GETAWAY

Key of A

This composition by Joe Sullivan was first recorded in 1933. It was one of Sullivan's most popular tunes while playing with Bing Crosby and later with his younger brother Bob's band, the Bobcats, which he joined in 1936.

This composition is, in its construction, similar to other tunes where the basic theme of the main chorus is descending chords. Morton's "Perfect Rag", for instance, is very similar.

I've put together a guitar arrangement using the first four sections of this six section piano extravaganza.

15. LITTLE ROCK GETAWAY

Joe Sullivan

Guitar arrangement by Lasse Johansson

Second section

First section repeated

AIN'T MISBEHAVIN'

Key of C

This is my version of the classic by Thomas "Fats" Waller. It's probably his most famous song. It first appeared 1929 in the Broadway hit *Hot Chocolates*. According to some sources, Waller wrote the score and his friend, Andy Razaf, the lyrics in less than an hour. Louis Armstrong played the trumpet and sang in the orchestra. He became the first singer to perform the song, at first from the bandstand but soon moving up onto the stage when the New York critics hailed his performance.

In 1934 Waller got a recording contract with RCA-Victor which helped him launch his fabulous career. His getting this contract was partly due to the fact that RCA, after purchasing the Victor company, had dropped Victor's biggest jazz star, Jelly Roll Morton. The chorus is well known to everybody but I have also included the seldom heard verse in my arrangement.

Thomas "Fats" Waller.

16. AIN'T MISBEHAVIN'

Fats Waller-Harry Brooks

Guitar arrangement by Lasse Johansson

Second section

Second section repeated

Second section repeated

HONG KONG BLUES

Key of A min

Composer Hoagland "Hoagy" Carmichael was a close friend of Bix Beiderbecke. He was the author of many well known compositions such as "Star Dust" and "Rockin' Chair".

"Hong Kong Blues", published in 1939, tells the story of an american sailor arrested in Hong Kong and in jail longing for his homeland. It was featured in the Casablanca sequel *To Have And Have Not* with Humphrey Bogart and Laureen Bacall. Hoagy Carmichel, himself, appears in the film, both singing and playing it.

In this arrangement, I've stayed away from using the "boom-chick" bass too much. The melodic and rhythmic "feel" of this tune is different when compared to the other material appearing in this collection.

17. HONG KONG BLUES

Hoagy Carmichael

Guitar arrangement by Lasse Johansson

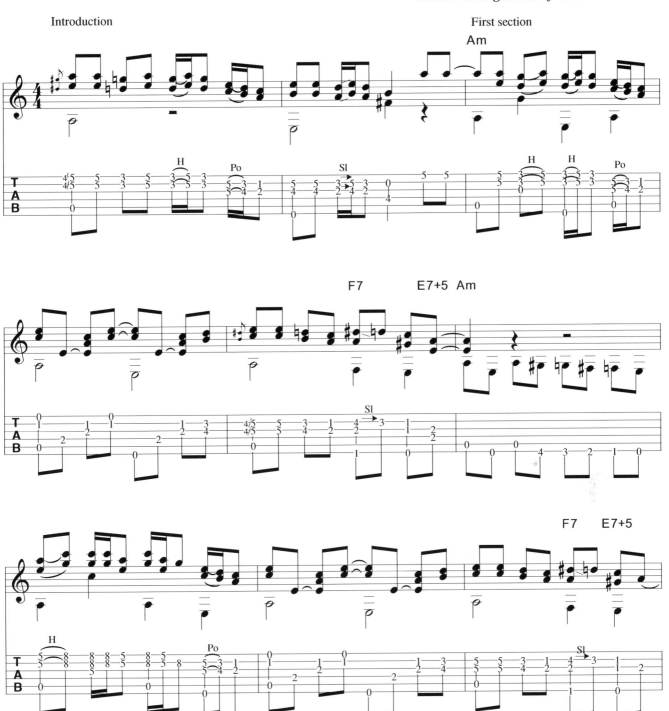

Second section repeated

114

Printed in Great Britain
by Amazon